RICHARD SCARRY'S

BIG

BUSY

STICKER &
ACTIVITY BOOK

STERLING CHILDREN'S BOOKS
New York

STERLING CHILDREN'S BOOKS
New York
An Imprint of Sterling Publishing
387 Park Avenue South
New York, NY 10016

ISBN 978-1-4027-7314-3

Distributed in Canada by Sterling Publishing
c/o Canadian Manda Group, 165 Dufferin Street
Toronto, Onatrio, Canada M6K 3H6
Distributed in the United Kingdom by GMC Distribution Services
Castle Place, 166 High Street, Lewes, East Sussex, England BN7 1XU
Distributed in Australia by Capricorn Link (Australia) Pty. Ltd.
P.O. Box 704, Windsor, NSW 2756, Australia

 jr sansevere

In association with JB Publishing, Inc.
41 River Terrace, New York, New York

For information about custom editions, special sales, and premium
and corporate purchases, please contact Sterling Special Sales at 800-805-5489
or specialsales@sterlingpublishing.com.

Printed in China

Lot#:
6 8 10 9 7
11/14

Ready for Work!

Can you help these busy workers find their hats?
You will find the hat stickers on sticker page A.
Place the correct hat on each worker's head. Thank you!

Mr. Frumble's Hat

Oh, no! Mr. Frumble was going to work when the wind blew away his hat! Place the hat sticker in the place below. Then follow the correct path to show Mr. Frumble which way to go to find his hat!

sticker page A

4

Motor Match

Place the correct sticker at the beginning of each row of pictures.
Then circle the picture that matches the sticker. You can do it!

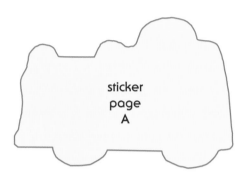  

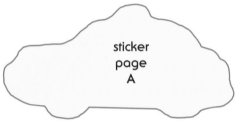  

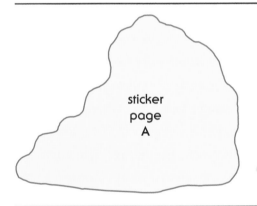  

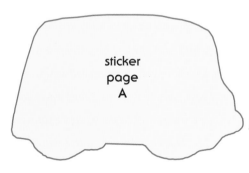  

5

Firefighter Fun

The Busytown firefighters are hard at work! Can you find 8 differences between the picture below and the one on the next page? Place star stickers from page **A** on all of the differences you find. Good luck!

Suit Up!

Help the firefighters get ready to go! Find all 8 words from the Word Bank hidden in the puzzle below. Look across and down!

```
H E L M E T
O B E L L R
S I R E N U
E G I A X C
B O O T S K
L A D D E R
```

WORD BANK

AX	HOSE
BELL	LADDER
BOOTS	SIREN
HELMET	TRUCK

Dot-to-Dot

Can you give Firefighter Squeeky a hand by connecting the dots from A to Z?
Then you can color what you've drawn. "Thanks!" says Squeeky.

Fire! Fire!

Oh, no! Kathleen Kitty's kitchen is on fire! Help the Busytown firefighters get there in time. First, change all of the red traffic lights to green ones by using the stickers on page A. Then draw a line through the city streets for the firefighters to follow.

START!

10

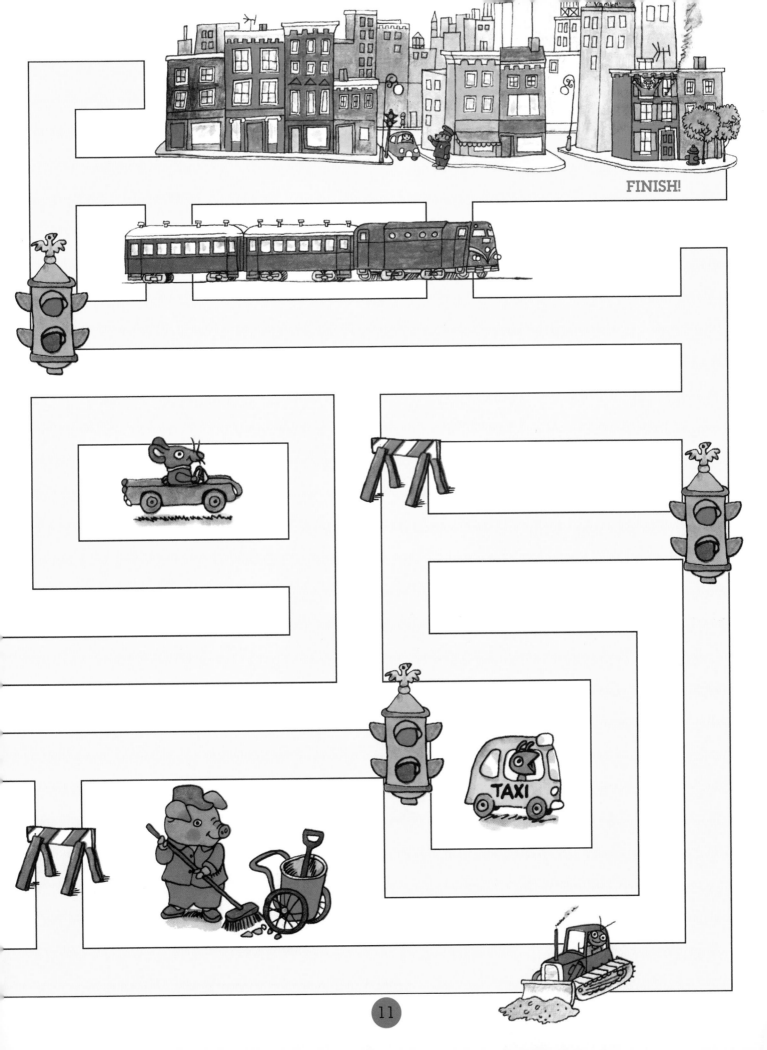

FINISH!

TAXI

Sergeant Murphy on Patrol

Color the picture of Sergeant Murphy below.
Then add some finishing touches using the stickers on page B.
It will look great!

A Sticky Suspect

Yikes! Somebody stole Ma Dog's cherry pies! Fortunately, she got a good look at the thief. Place the police sketch sticker into the box below and use it to help Sergeant Murphy pick out the suspect from the line-up below.

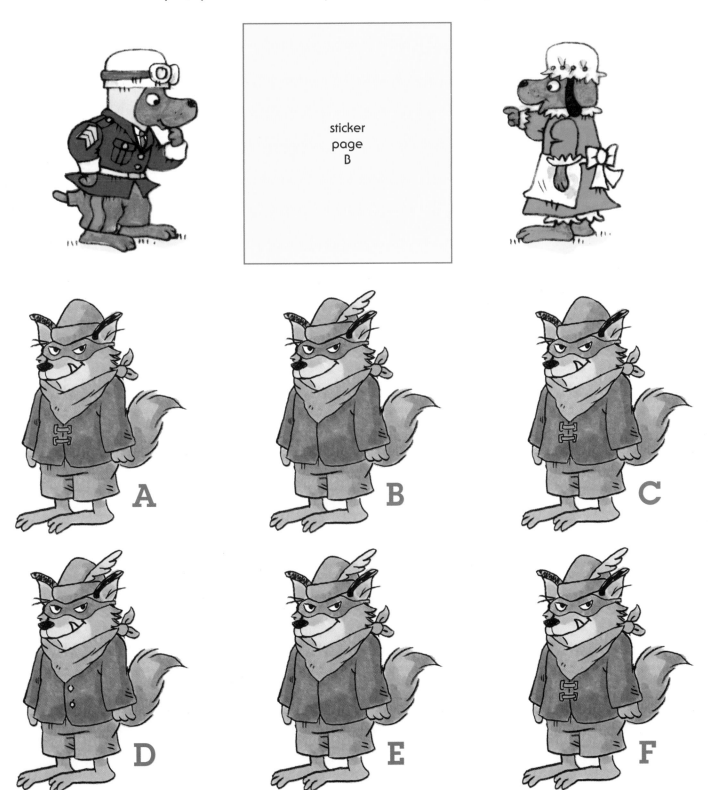

sticker page B

A   B   C

D   E   F

Catch the Crooks!

You need a friend to play this game. Each player takes a turn connecting two neighboring dots with a straight line. You can go up and down and side to side, but not diagonally. Try to be the player who makes a box by adding the last line of a square. When you do, write your initial in the box and take an extra turn. Each plain square is 1 point; a square with a crook in it is 2 points. The player with the highest score wins!

Use the crook stickers found on page B to set up the game grid on page 15. Place the stickers between the dots just like in the game board below.

Have fun! Good luck!

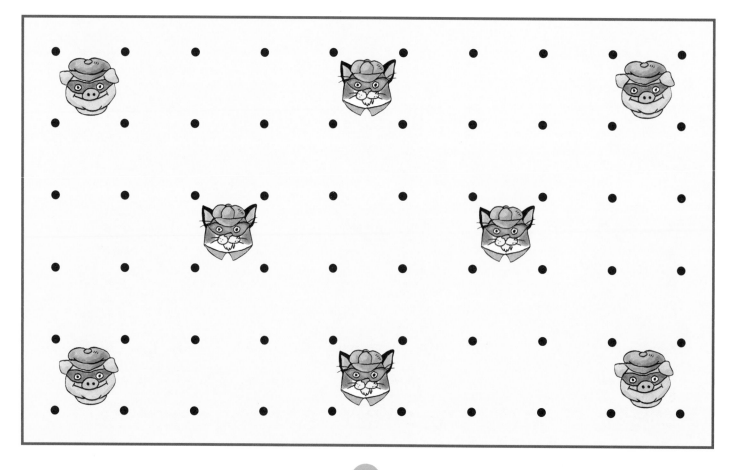

14

Dizzy Drivers

These drivers have lost their vehicles! Help find them by first following the line from each driver to the numbered box at the end of the line. Then place the correct vehicle sticker from page B for each driver over the numbered space.

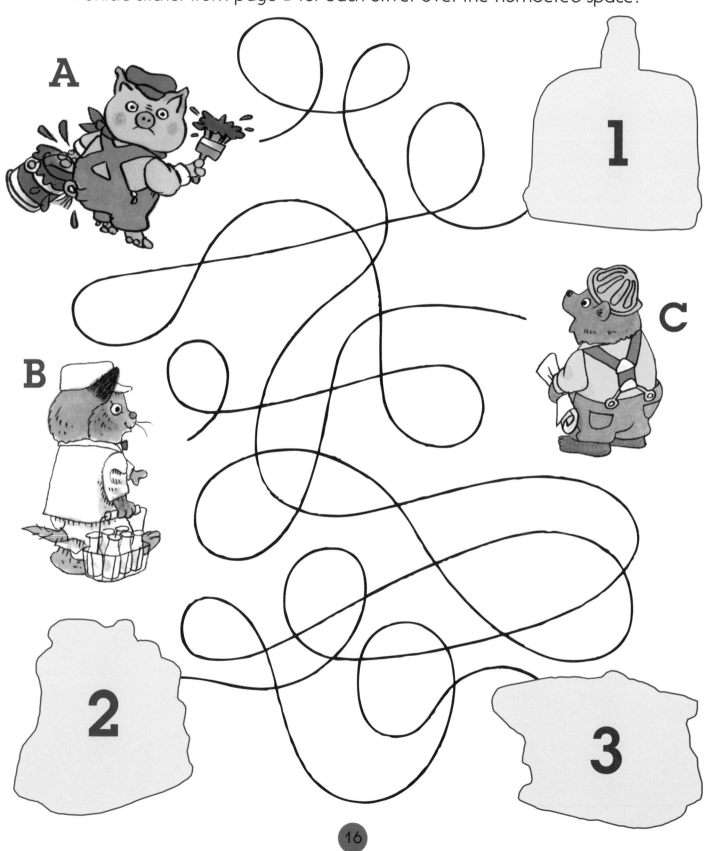

Ready for Work! p. 3

Mr. Frumble's Hat
p. 4

Motor Match p. 5

Firefighter Fun p. 6-7

Fire! Fire!
p. 10-11

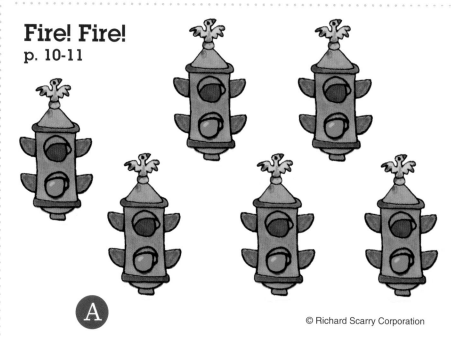

A

Sergeant Murphy on Patrol p. 12

A Sticky Suspect p. 13

Catch the Crooks! p. 14-15

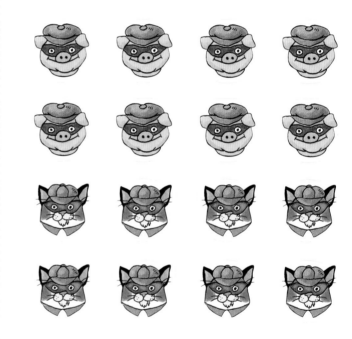

Dizzy Drivers p. 16

Mail Match-Up p. 17

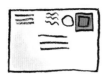  

Sticky Stamps p. 19

Postwoman Patty's Busy Day p. 20-21

 BARBER SNIP-SNIP BUSYTOWN, U.S.A.

 HARRY'S HARDWARE BUSYTOWN, U.S.A.

 Edgar's Eyeglasses Busytown, U.S.A.

 DORIS THE FLORIST BUSYTOWN, U.S.A.

 Police Chief Charlie Busytown, U.S.A.

What Comes Next? p. 22

Gas and Go! p. 23

C

© Richard Scarry Corporation

Motor Match p. 25

Inside, Outside
p. 26

A Visit to the Doctor p. 28

Check-Up p. 32

(D)

Mail Match-Up

Can you help Postman Pig sort the mail? Place the envelope stickers from sticker page C into the correct bins below by matching the color of the stamp on each letter to the color of the bin. Postman Pig says "Thank You!"

17

Dot-to-Dot

Connect the dots from 1 to 29 to help Lowly mail his letter.
Then finish coloring the picture.

Sticky Stamps

Help Huckle mail his letters by placing the stamp with the correct amount onto each envelope. Stamp stickers can be found on sticker page C.

1¢ stamp

Lowly Worm
Busytown, U.S.A.

5¢ stamp

Nigel Fox
London, England

10¢

10¢ stamp

Susie Dingo
Sydney, Australia

MAIL

Postwoman Patty's Busy Day

Help Postwoman Patty on her mail route by following the correct path through Busytown. Make sure everyone gets their mail by placing the mail stickers on the correct buildings. Mail stickers can be found on sticker page C.

START!

HARDWARE

POLICE

20

BARBER SNIP SNIP

Eyeglasses

FLORIST

FINISH!

POST OFFICE

What Comes Next?

Can you place the shape that comes next on the question mark at the end of each sequence? Shape stickers can be found on sticker page C.

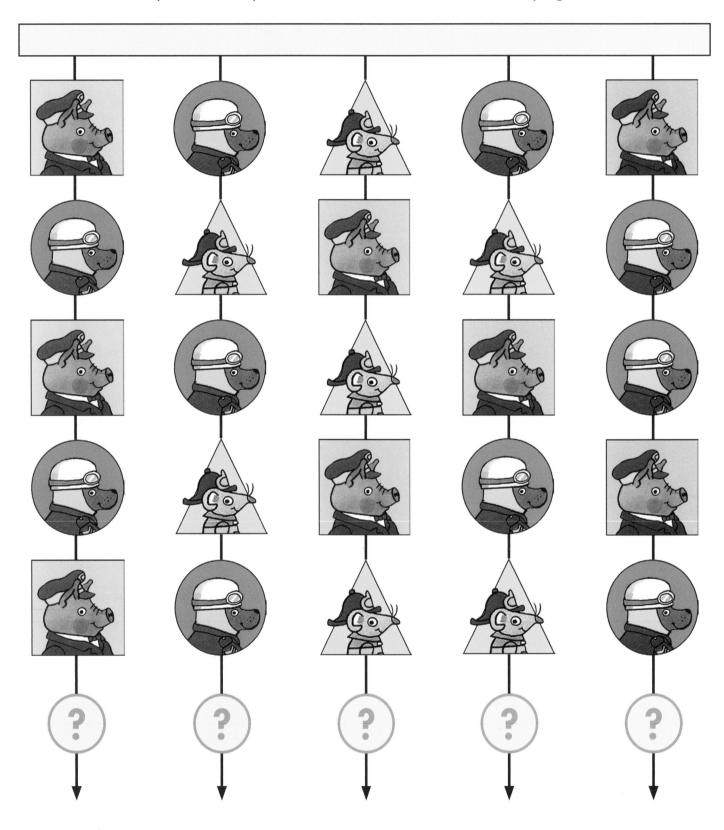

Gas and Go!

Greasy George is filling all of the Busytown cars with gas, but he doesn't know which kind of gas goes in each car. Can you help him? Match the symbol on each gas pump with the correct car sticker. Stickers can be found on page C.

Cement Mixer Mix-Up

Mixer Mouse has mixed up all of the words! See if you can unscramble them. Use the Word Bank below if you need a hint.

TRID

1) _____

ROWK

2) _____

LIDUB

3) _____

LEOH

4) _____

ARDO

5) _____

CRTUK

6) _____

WORD BANK
BUILD
DIRT
HOLE
ROAD
TRUCK
WORK

24

Motor Match

Place the correct sticker at the beginning of each row of pictures.
Then circle the picture that matches the sticker.

sticker page D		
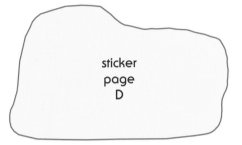		
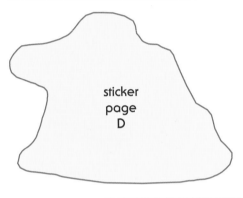		
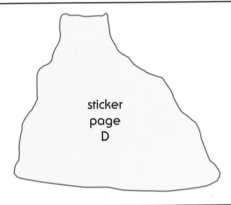		
sticker page D		

25

Inside, Outside

Place a BLUE star sticker on the people who work OUTSIDE. Place a RED star sticker on the people who work INSIDE. Star stickers can be found on page D.

Go, Flo, Go!

Dingo Dog is driving too fast! Help Deputy Flo choose the best path through the traffic to catch up to him!

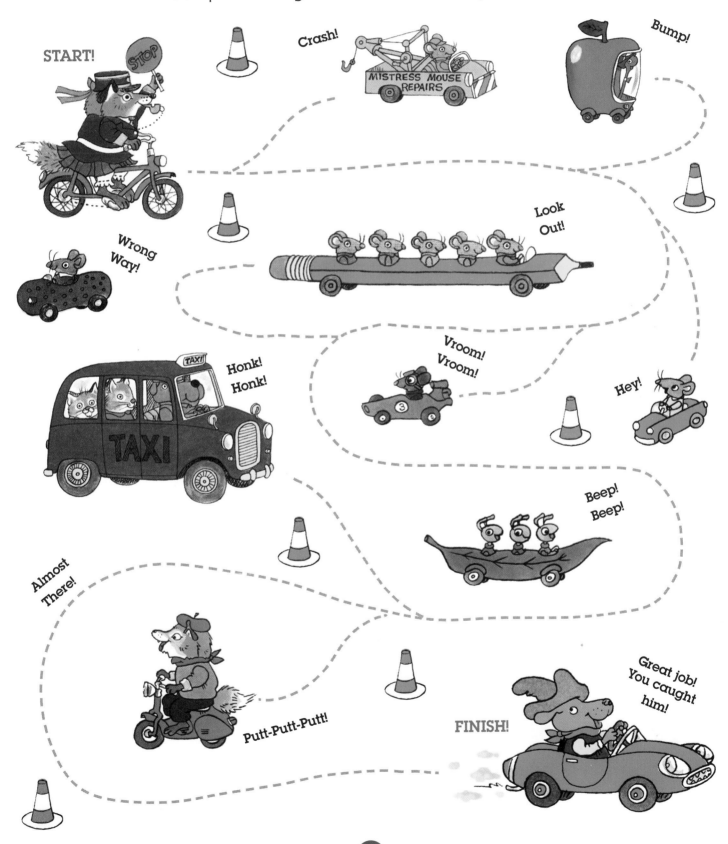

START!

Crash!

MISTRESS MOUSE REPAIRS

Bump!

Wrong Way!

Look Out!

Honk! Honk!

TAXI

Vroom! Vroom!

Hey!

Beep! Beep!

Almost There!

Putt-Putt-Putt!

FINISH!

Great job! You caught him!

27

A Visit to the Doctor

Huckle is having a check-up at Dr. Bones.
Can you color this picture, and add some stickers from page D?

Head to Feet

It's time to visit the doctor! Find the parts of the body from the Word Bank hidden in the puzzle below. Look across and down!

WORD BANK
ARMS
BELLY
EARS
EYES
FEET
HANDS
HEAD
LEGS
MOUTH
NOSE

S	M	O	U	T	H
A	F	Y	A	H	A
B	E	L	L	Y	N
E	E	H	E	A	D
Y	T	H	G	R	S
E	A	R	S	M	H
S	H	N	O	S	E

29

Rescue Roundabout

Help the Busytown ambulance get to the hospital on time!
Draw a line through the city streets for the ambulance to follow.

START!

GO RIGHT

TV

WILLIAM TELL

TAXI

FINISH!

HOSPITAL

31

Check-Up

It's time for Nicky's yearly check-up with the doctor. See if you can find six things wrong with the picture below. Place bandage stickers on the things that are wrong. The stickers can be found on page D.

Marina Match p. 33

Flight Check p. 38-39

Moon Mission p. 40

E

Land, Sea, and Air p. 36-37

Mixing Colors p. 44

 purple  pink  gray  orange  green

Color Confusion p. 45

Musical March
p. 46

Apple Picking p. 54

(G)

Farmer's Market
p. 49

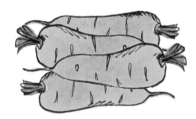
carrots

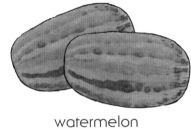
potatoes

watermelon

tomatoes

onions

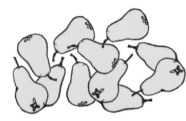
apples

pears

lettuce

Where's My Cow? p. 50

What Comes Next? p. 51

Pattern Planting p. 55

Ⓗ

© Richard Scarry Corporation

Marina Match

Place the correct sticker at the beginning of each row of pictures.
Then circle the picture that matches the sticker.

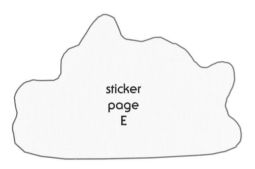  

sticker page E

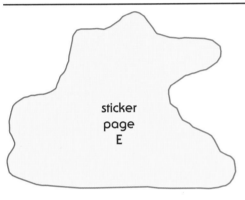  

sticker page E

sticker page E

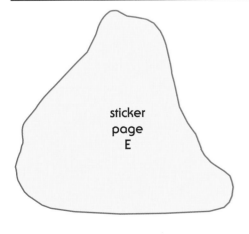  

sticker page E

33

Uncle Willy's Busy Day

Can you help Uncle Willy by finding the objects listed below hidden in the picture? Place a star sticker on each object you find. Then color the picture. The stickers can be found on page E.

CHEESE	MUSHROOM	PIZZA SLICE
FISH	OVERALLS	ROLLER SKATE
ICE CREAM	PIE	SHEEP

Dot-to-Dot

Connect the dots from 1-23 to see what's there. Then finish coloring the picture.

Land, Sea, and Air

Use the stickers found on page **F** to make your own seaside scene!

Flight Check

The airport is a busy place! See if you can spot 8 differences between the picture below and the one on page 39. Place the star stickers from sticker page **E** on all of the differences you find!

Moon Mission

Connect the dots from 1 to 24 to help the astronauts get to the moon. Then color the picture and use the star stickers on sticker page **E** to add a starry sky.

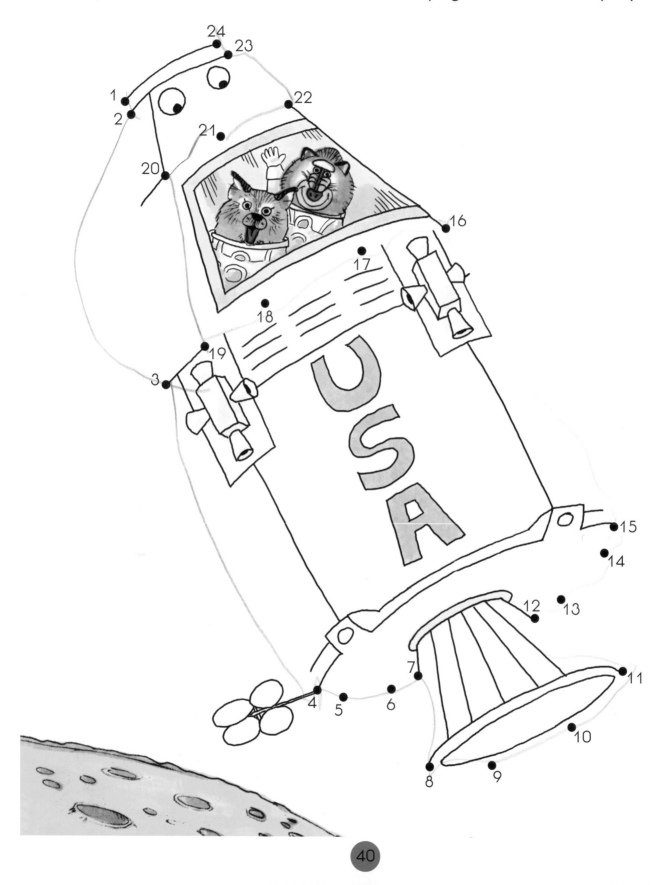

A Long Way Home

Now the astronauts need to get back to Earth. Can you help them? First, help them find Earth by placing the sticker in the correct spot. Then follow the path through the stars to lead them home!

sticker page E

Colorful Crossword

Help Mr. Paint Pig by using the colored clues to fill in the puzzle with the correct color names. Look at the Word Bank if you need a hint.

WORD BANK

BLACK   PURPLE
BLUE   RED
GREEN   WHITE
ORANGE   YELLOW

Color by Number

Help Mr. Paint Pig color the picture. Fill in each numbered space with the corresponding color.

1 = yellow   2 = blue   3 = green

4 = brown   5 = red   6 = black

Mixing Colors

Help Huckle mix colors! Place the correct color sticker that would result from each color pair. Then write the name of the new color on the line below. The paint blob stickers can be found on sticker page G.

red yellow ?

blue yellow ?

red blue ?

red white ?

black white ?

44

Color Confusion

Mr. Paint Pig has mixed up his paintbrushes! Help him out by placing the correct brush into each can of paint. The paintbrush stickers can be found on sticker page **G**. Please don't drip anywhere!

WHITE

BLACK

RED

BLUE

GREEN

YELLOW

ORANGE

PINK

PURPLE

BROWN

Musical March

Place the musician who comes next at the end of each row.
Musican stickers can be found on sticker page G.

Band Practice

It's time for Huckle's class orchestra to practice. See if you can find all of their instruments hidden in the puzzle. Look across and down.

DRUM

FLUTE

CELLO

GUITAR

HARP

VIOLIN

PIANO

TUBA

F	G	H	A	R	P	P
L	U	F	I	P	V	I
U	I	D	D	I	I	I
T	T	U	B	A	O	I
E	A	L	E	N	L	
D	R	U	M	O	I	
C	E	L	L	O	N	

47

Dot-to-Dot

Connect the dots from 1 to 34 to see what instrument Parade Pig is playing.
Then color the picture.

A Day at the Farm p. 52-53

I

Flower Tic-Tac-Toe p. 56-57

J

Huckle's Busy Day p. 58-59

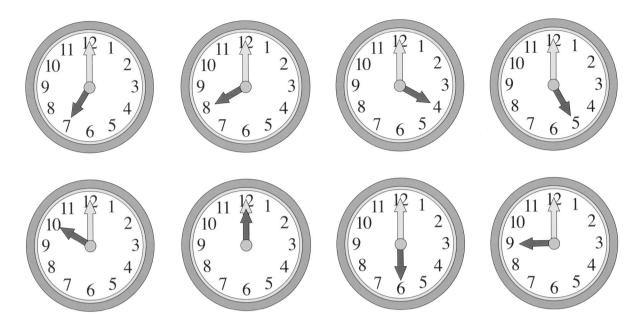

School Days p. 60-61

Cookie Capture! p. 66-67

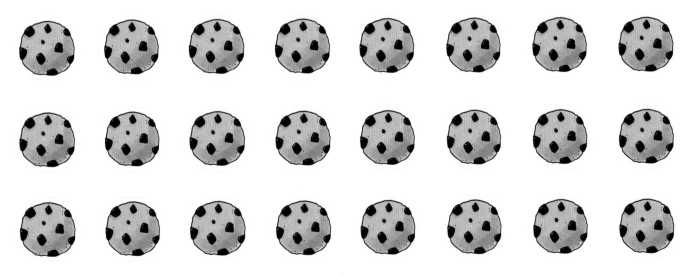

K

L

Farmer's Market

Help Farmer Alfalfa set up his stand for the farmer's market by placing the fruits and vegetables in their correct boxes. The stickers for this activity can be found on sticker page H.

apples

carrots

lettuce

onions

pears

potatoes

tomatoes

watermelon

49

Where's My Cow?

Farmer Cat's cow has wandered off and he needs your help to find her! First, place the picture of his cow into the box below and use it to help Farmer Cat pick out the correct cow from the herd below. When you find the matching cow, circle it.

sticker
page
H

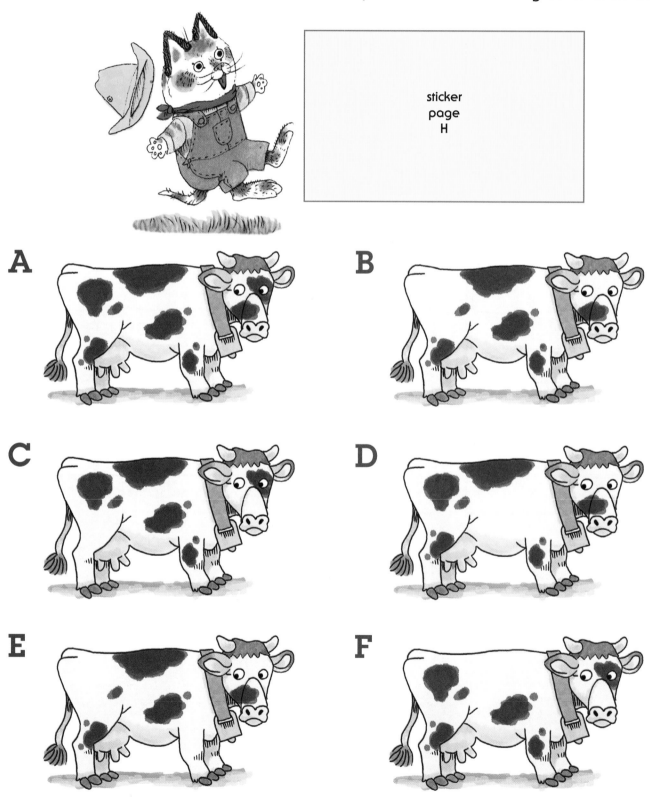

A

B

C

D

E

F

What Comes Next?

Place the shape that comes next on the question mark at the end of each sequence.
Shape stickers can be found on sticker page H.

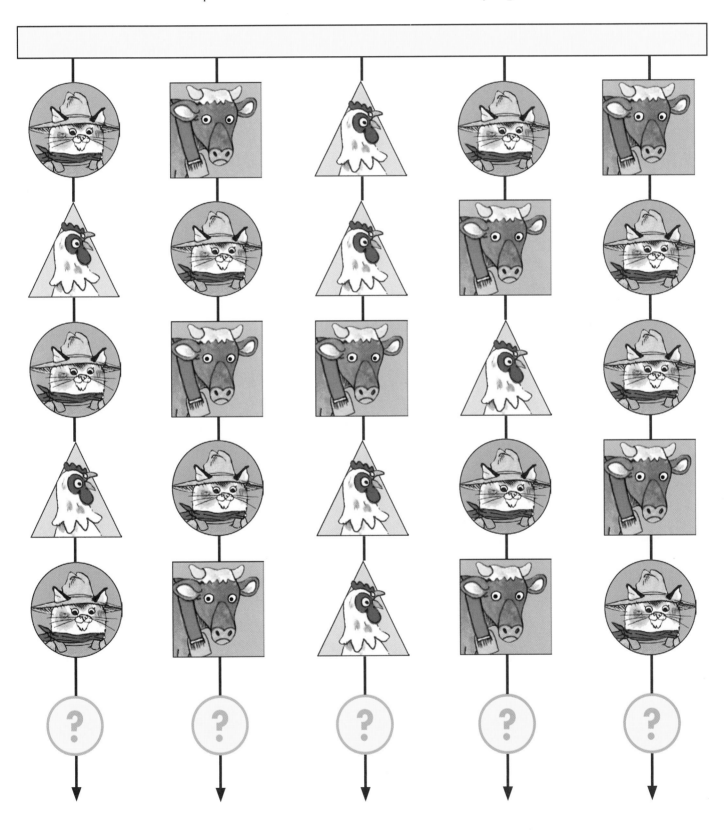

A Day at the Farm

Use the stickers found on page 1 to make your own farm scene! Have fun!

Apple Picking

Huckle and Sally want to pick apples, but there are none on the tree! First, color the picture. Then add some apples to the scene using the stickers on page G.

54

Pattern Planting

Help Mother Cat plant her garden. Place the flower that comes next at the end of each sequence. The flower stickers can be found on sticker page H.

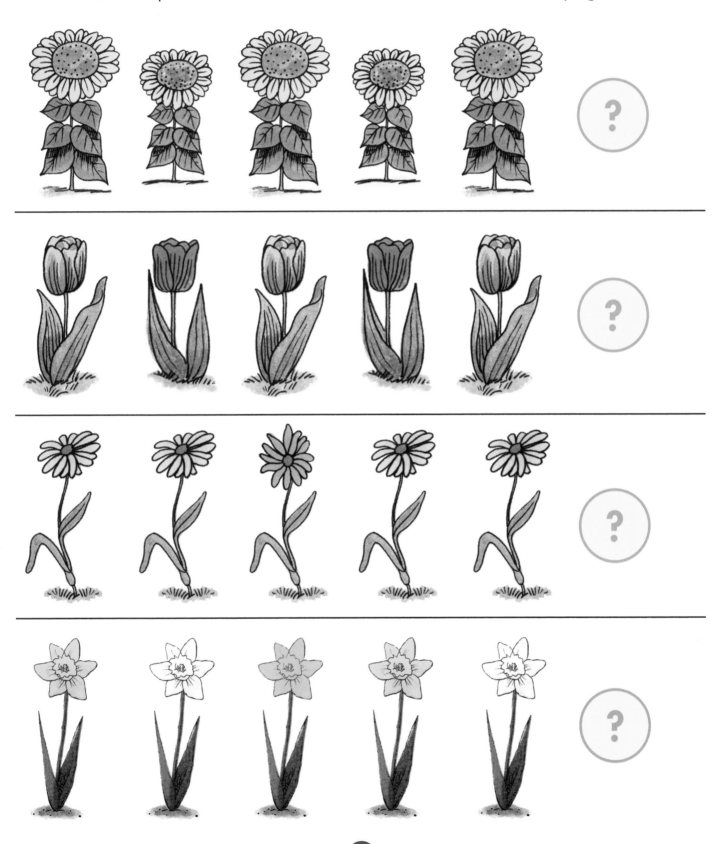

Flower Tic-Tac-Toe

You need a friend to play this game. Using the flower stickers on page J, try to be the first one to get three flowers in a row going across, down, or diagonally. Good luck!

57

Huckle's Busy Day

Help Huckle go through his day by pairing the correct clock sticker with each picture. The clock stickers can be found on sticker page K.

sticker page K

At **7 o'clock** Huckle gets out of bed.

sticker page K

At **8 o'clock** he eats breakfast.

sticker page K

At **10 o'clock** he goes shopping with Mother Cat.

sticker page K

12 o'clock is noontime. Huckle and Lowly eat lunch.

58

At **4 o'clock** they watch television.

sticker page K

At **5 o'clock** it is time to eat supper.

sticker page K

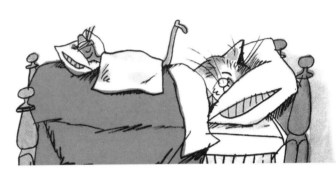

At **6 o'clock** Father Cat gives Huckle his bath.

sticker page K

By **9 o'clock** Huckle is fast asleep. Good night, Huckle!

sticker page K

School Days

Welcome to Miss Honey's class! See if you can spot 8 differences between the picture below and the one on page 61. Place the star stickers from sticker page K on all of the differences you find!

ABC's

Help Miss Honey's class complete the alphabet chart by placing each sticker next to the letter it starts with. The stickers can be found on sticker page L. You can do it!

LEARNING THE
ALPHABET
Aa Bb Cc Dd Ee Ff Gg Hh Ii Jj Kk Ll
Mm Nn Oo Pp Qq Rr Ss Tt Uu Vv Ww Xx Yy Zz

Aa	Bb
Cc	Dd
Ee	Ff

Gg	Hh
Ii	Jj
Kk	Ll
Mm	Nn
Oo	Pp

Next page...

Qq	Rr
Ss	Tt
Uu	Vv
Ww	Xx
Yy	Zz

Make a Cake p. 65

A Busy Bakery p. 68-69

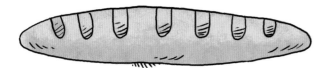

Brownie's Busy Day p. 70-71

Sawdust's Search p. 72

Tools of the Trade
p. 74

O

Plumbing Puzzle p. 75

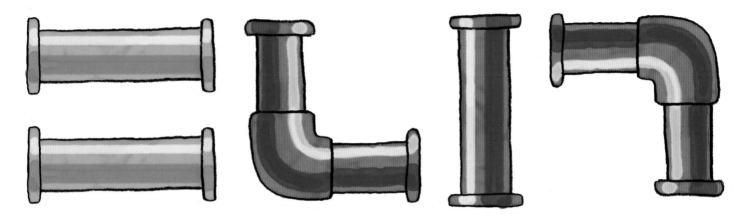

Mr. Fix-It's Busy Day p. 76-77

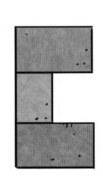

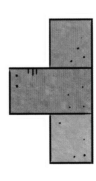

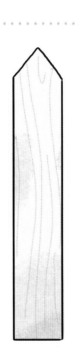

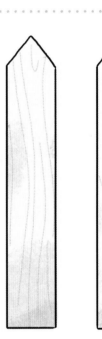

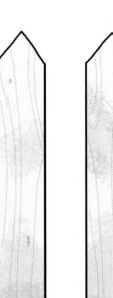

P

Make a Cake

Able Baker Charlie has made a cake and he needs your help to finish it! First, color the cake. Then use the stickers found on sticker page M to decorate it.

Cookie Capture!

You need a friend to play this game. Each player takes a turn connecting two neighboring dots with a straight line. You can go up and down and side to side, but not diagonally. Try to be the player who makes a box by adding the last line of a square. When you do, write your initial in the box and take an extra turn. Each plain square is 1 point; a square with a cookie in it is 2 points. The player with the highest score wins!

Use the cookie stickers found on page K to set up the game grid on page 67. Place the stickers between the dots just like in the game board below.

Good luck! Have fun!

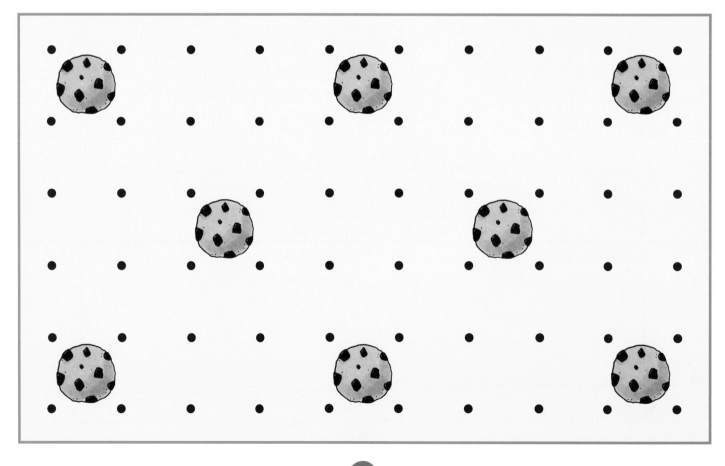

66

A Busy Bakery

Humperdink has a lot of orders to fill. Help him out by placing the correct number of baked goods into each box. The baked goods stickers can be found on page N.

6 cupcakes

2 loaves of bread

1 pie

8 doughnuts

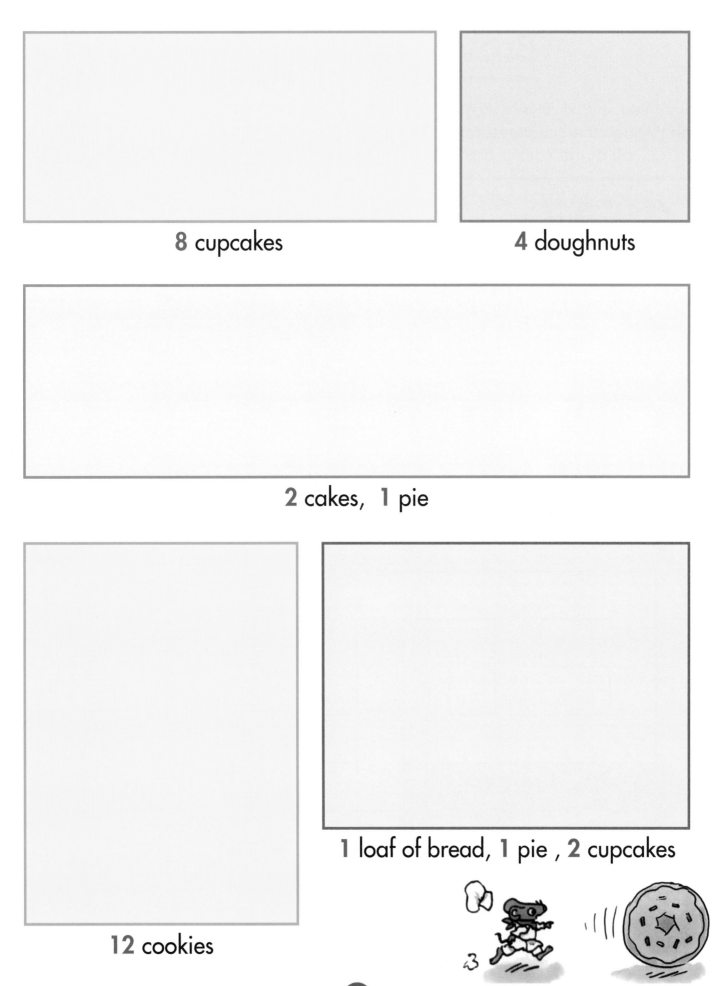

8 cupcakes

4 doughnuts

2 cakes, 1 pie

12 cookies

1 loaf of bread, 1 pie , 2 cupcakes

69

Brownie's Busy Day

Brownie the taxi driver takes people wherever they want to go in Busytown. Draw a line through the city streets for him to follow. Make sure you drop all of his passengers off at the correct places. Passenger stickers can be found on page O.

Mother Cat is going to the grocery store.

Miss Dog is going to the bank.

Marvin is going to the newstand.

Mother Pig is going to the bakery.

Huckle is going to the library.

TAXI

START!

GROCERIES

BANK

70

NEWS

BAKERY

FINISH!

PUBLIC LIBRARY

71

Sawdust's Search

Sawdust the carpenter is looking for his tools! Help him find their names from the Word Bank in the puzzle below. Then put the tool stickers found on sticker page O over their names at the bottom of the page.

```
W R E N C H
S S C D R A
A E W R D M
W R I I V M
N A I L S E
R R U L E R
```

WORD BANK:

DRILL

HAMMER

NAILS

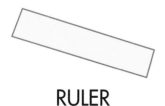
RULER

SAW

WRENCH

72

Dot-to-Dot

Connect the dots from 1 to 15 to see what Sawdust is building!
Finish coloring the picture when you're done!

Tools of the Trade

Mr. Fix-It needs to get his toolbox ready for his next job. Look at the stickers on sticker page O. Stick the 6 items that belong in a toolbox into toolbox below.

Plumbing Puzzle

Pipe the plumber has a problem! Use the pipe stickers found on page P to connect the pipes together. Green must connect to green and purple connects to purple.

Mr. Fix-It's Busy Day

Father Cat has asked Mr. Fix-It to do some repairs around the house. Use the stickers found on sticker page P to help Mr. Fix-It get the job done!

First, please repair the chimney.

Next, please mend the fence by replacing the missing boards.

Then, please replace the broken glass.

Finally, please hang up the new front door.

Good job!
Thank you so much!

 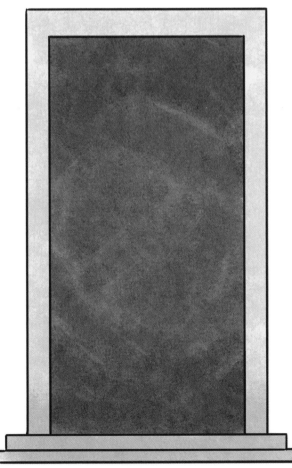  

Grocer Cat's Crossword

Use the picture clues to fill in the puzzle with some of the things Grocer Cat sells in his store. Look at the Word Bank if you need a hint.

WORD BANK

APPLES   EGGS

BREAD   LETTUCE

BUTTER   MILK

Check-Out

Can you help Mother Pig shop for groceries? Find the items on her list on sticker page Q, then place them on the check-out counter.

Shopping List:
apples   ice cream
bread   jam
cheese   milk
eggs   oranges

Traffic Patterns

Place the car that comes next at the end of each row.
Car stickers can be found on sticker page Q. Toot! Toot!

Check-Out p. 79

Traffic Patterns p. 80

Picture Perfect p. 81

Q

A Busy Day in Busytown p. 82-83

MAIL

TAXI

HOT DOGS

1

Let's Recycle p. 84

Super Scoopers p. 85

Use the extra stickers to build your own ice cream cones!

S

Picnic Lunch p.87

A Day at the Beach p. 88-89

★ ★ ★ ★ ★ ★ ★ ★

★ ★ ★ ★ ★ ★ ★ ★

We're extra stickers!

T

Picture Perfect

Use the stickers found on sticker page Q to fill in the missing pieces of the picture.

A Busy Day in Busytown

Use the stickers found on page R to make your own street scene! Have fun!

ART GALLERY

E.K BOOK SHOP

Let's Recycle

Huckle wants to recycle his old bottles, cans, and paper. Sort the stickers found on page S into their proper containers. Thank you!

GLASS

PAPER

CANS

Super Scoopers

Scoopy the ice cream man has lots of frozen treats. Look at the pattern of scoops on each cone and top each one off with the flavor that comes next.
Ice cream stickers can be found on sticker page S. No dripping, please!

Day Off!

The Pig family is going on a picnic! Follow the correct path to the picnic area.
Don't let the ants ruin their day!

START!

FINISH!

Picnic Lunch

Help the Pig family get their basket ready for their picnic. Look at the stickers on sticker page T. Stick the 9 items that belong on a picnic into the basket below.

A Day at the Beach

Everyone is having a great time at the beach! See if you can spot 8 differences between the picture below and the one on page 89. Place the star stickers from sticker page T on all of the differences you find!

EAT BRUNO'S HOT DOGS

DRINK WATER

BRUNO'S HOT DOGS

LIFE GUARD

EAT BRUNO'S HOT DOGS

DRINK WATER

BRUNO'S HOT DOGS

LIFE GUARD

LIFE GUARD

Shells and Starfish

You need a friend to play this game. One player chooses shells and the other chooses starfish. Using the shell and starfish stickers on page U, try to be the first one to get three of their symbol in a row going across, down, or diagonally. Good luck!

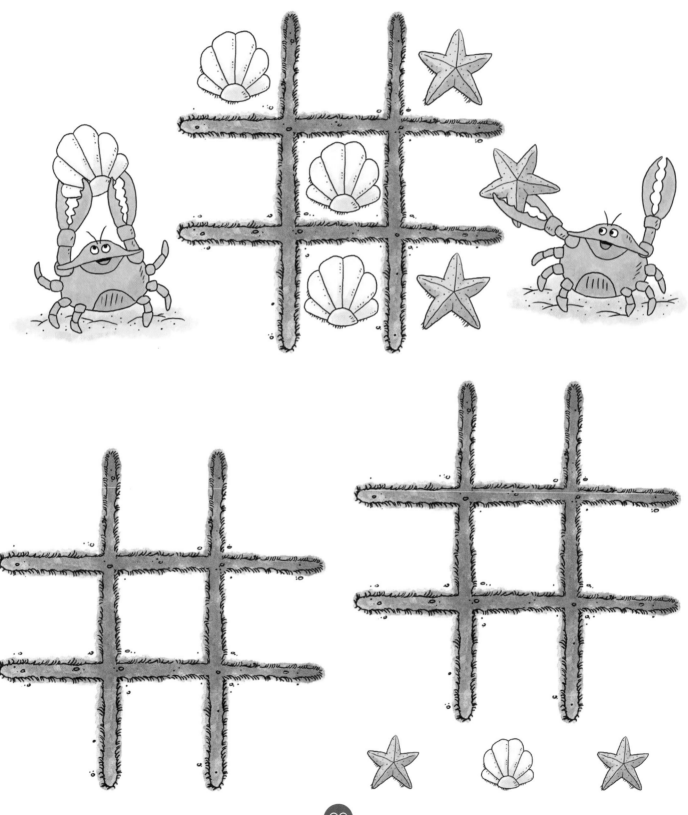

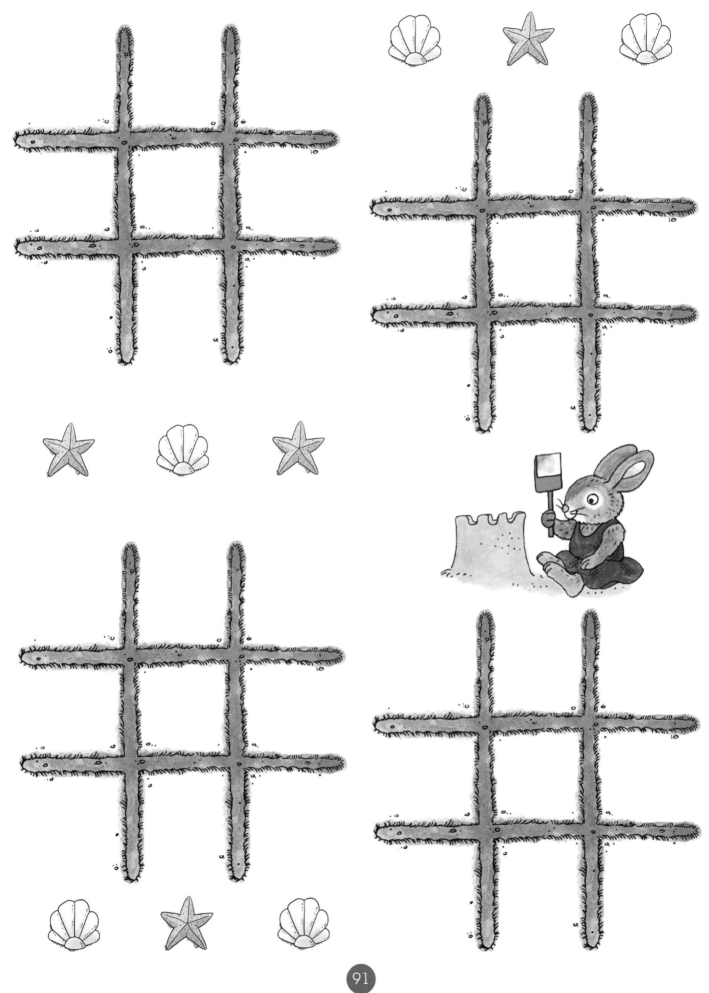

Answers (Just in case you need help!)

Motor Match p. 5

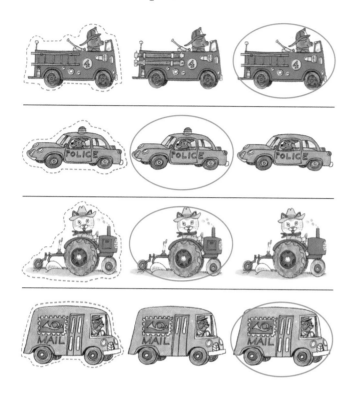

Firefighter Fun p. 6-7

The 8 differences are:
1) The pig on ladder has the top of his hat missing.
2) There is a mouse in a teapot car near the firehouse.
3) The pig on the truck is wearing a helmet instead of a pan.
4) The roadblock near the manhole is missing.
5) The word "chief" is missing from the side of the car.
6) The bell on the firetruck is missing.
7) The number on the truck is "2".
8) There is a bug news van instead of a mouse in the lower right corner.

Suit Up! p. 8

A Sticky Suspect p. 13

Suspect **F** matches the sticker.

Dizzy Drivers p. 16

A = 2   B = 1   C = 3

What Comes Next? p. 22

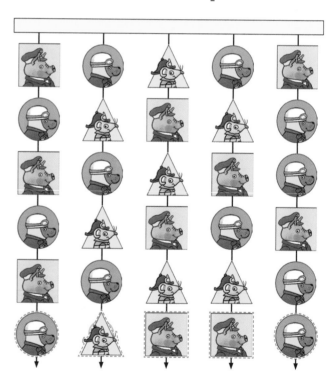

Cement Mixer Mix-Up p. 24

1) DIRT   3) BUILD   5) ROAD
2) WORK   4) HOLE   6) TRUCK

92

Motor Match p. 25

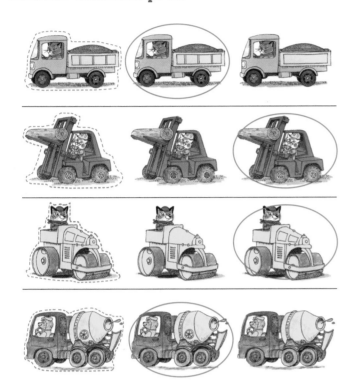

Head to Feet p. 29

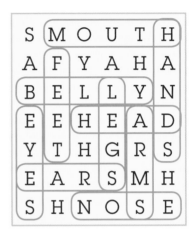

Check-Up p. 32

The 6 things wrong with the picture are:
1) The clock is backward.
2) There is an ice cream cone in the cabinet on the wall.
3) There is a chick in the cabinet on the wall
4) The doctor's diploma is upside down.
5) The jar on the counter has pickles in it.
6) There is a chicken under the table.

Marina Match p. 33

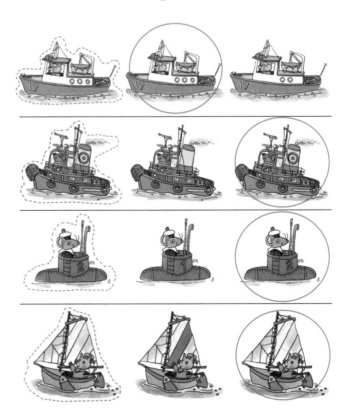

Inside, Outside p. 26

Uncle Willy's Busy Day p. 34

Flight Check p. 38-39

The 8 differences are:
1) The helicopter is facing to the left.
2) There is a hot air balloon instead of a parachute.
3) The small yellow plane is replaced with a blue plane.
4) The arrow on top of the tower is facing to the right.
5) The luggage man near the front of the plane is missing.
6) The blue suitcase near the front of the plane has been replaced with a brown one.
7) There is a rabbit girl on the stairs.
8) The green suitcase on the end of the luggage cart is missing.

Colorful Crossword p. 42

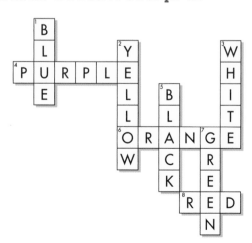

Mixing Colors p. 44

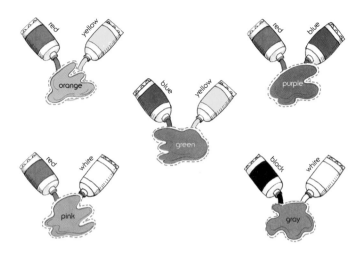

Musical March p. 46

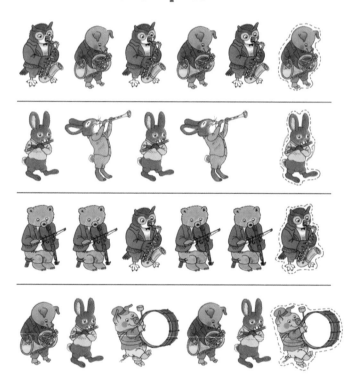

Band Practice p. 47

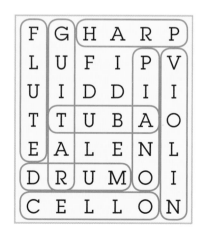

94

Where's My Cow? p. 50

Cow **C** matches the sticker.

What Comes Next? p. 51

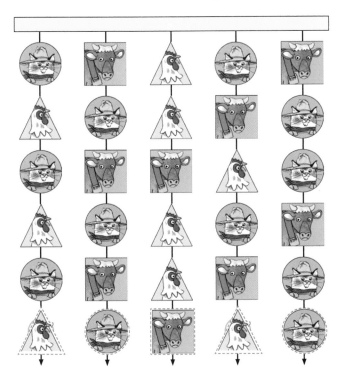

Pattern Planting p. 55

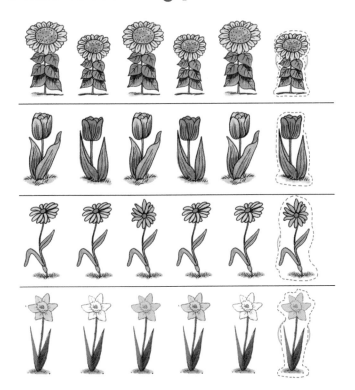

School Days p. 60-61

The 8 differences are:
1) The "10" on the number chart is missing.
2) The math problem on the board is "4 + 2" instead of "4 + 4".
3) There is an eraser by the chalkboard.
4) The flowers on the desk are red.
5) The book on the desk is blue.
6) The red pen on the teacher's desk is missing.
7) There is a bottle of paste on the small desk on the right.
8) The mouse has a pear in his wagon.

Sawdust's Search p. 72

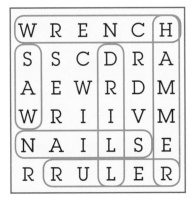

Plumbing Puzzle p. 75

Grocer Cat's Crossword p. 78

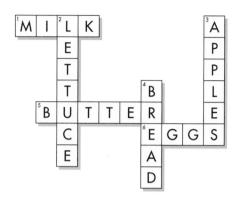

Traffic Patterns p. 80

Super Scoopers p. 85

A Day at the Beach p. 88-89

The 8 differences are:
1) The blimp is facing to the right.
2) There is a cloud in front of the sun.
3) The small green airplane is missing.
4) There is a hippo girl near the water in the background.
5) There is a sleeping man next to the lifeguard instead of a rabbit and a sandcastle.
6) There is a shovel next to Father Pig instead of a pail.
7) There is a pig with a pail next to the crab instead of a rabbit with a seashell.
8) The starfish is near the pig with the pail instead of near the water.

Are you all finished? Great job! We'll see you next time!

96